VOL. 142

KINGS O   N

Cover photo courtesy of RCA Records

ISBN 978-1-4584-0737-5

7777 W. BLUEMOUND RD. P.O. BOX 13819 MILWAUKEE, WI 53213

In Australia Contact:
Hal Leonard Australia Pty. Ltd.
4 Lentara Court
Cheltenham, Victoria, 3192 Australia
Email: ausadmin@halleonard.com.au

Visit Hal Leonard Online at
www.halleonard.com

GUITAR NOTATION LEGEND

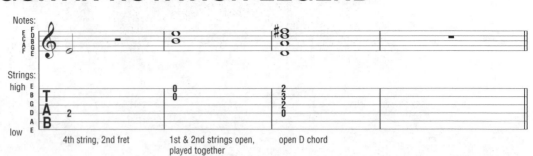

THE MUSICAL STAFF shows pitches and rhythms and is divided by bar lines into measures. Pitches are named after the first seven letters of the alphabet.

TABLATURE graphically represents the guitar fingerboard. Each horizontal line represents a string, and each number represents a fret.

4th string, 2nd fret   1st & 2nd strings open, played together   open D chord

HALF-STEP BEND: Strike the note and bend up 1/2 step.

BEND AND RELEASE: Strike the note and bend up as indicated, then release back to the original note. Only the first note is struck.

HAMMER-ON: Strike the first (lower) note with one finger, then sound the higher note (on the same string) with another finger by fretting it without picking.

TRILL: Very rapidly alternate between the notes indicated by continuously hammering on and pulling off.

TREMOLO PICKING: The note is picked as rapidly and continuously as possible.

WHOLE-STEP BEND: Strike the note and bend up one step.

PRE-BEND: Bend the note as indicated, then strike it.

PULL-OFF: Place both fingers on the notes to be sounded. Strike the first note and without picking, pull the finger off to sound the second (lower) note.

TAPPING: Hammer ("tap") the fret indicated with the pick-hand index or middle finger and pull off to the note fretted by the fret hand.

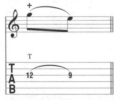

VIBRATO BAR DIVE AND RETURN: The pitch of the note or chord is dropped a specified number of steps (in rhythm), then returned to the original pitch.

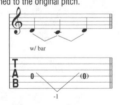

GRACE NOTE BEND: Strike the note and immediately bend up as indicated.

VIBRATO: The string is vibrated by rapidly bending and releasing the note with the fretting hand.

LEGATO SLIDE: Strike the first note and then slide the same fret-hand finger up or down to the second note. The second note is not struck.

NATURAL HARMONIC: Strike the note while the fret-hand lightly touches the string directly over the fret indicated.

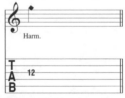

VIBRATO BAR SCOOP: Depress the bar just before striking the note, then quickly release the bar.

SLIGHT (MICROTONE) BEND: Strike the note and bend up 1/4 step.

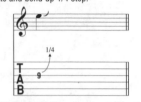

PALM MUTING: The note is partially muted by the pick hand lightly touching the string(s) just before the bridge.

SHIFT SLIDE: Same as legato slide, except the second note is struck.

PINCH HARMONIC: The note is fretted normally and a harmonic is produced by adding the edge of the thumb or the tip of the index finger of the pick hand to the normal pick attack.

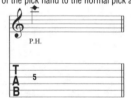

VIBRATO BAR DIP: Strike the note and then immediately drop a specified number of steps, then release back to the original pitch.

Additional Musical Definitions

(*accent*) • Accentuate note (play it louder).

(*staccato*) • Play the note short.

D.S. al Coda • Go back to the sign (𝄋), then play until the measure marked "***To Coda***," then skip to the section labelled "**Coda**."

D.C. al Fine • Go back to the beginning of the song and play until the measure marked "***Fine***" (end).

Fill • Label used to identify a brief melodic figure which is to be inserted into the arrangement.

N.C. • Harmony is implied.

• Repeat measures between signs.

• When a repeated section has different endings, play the first ending only the first time and the second ending only the second time.

CONTENTS

The Bucket

Words and Music by Caleb Followill, Nathan Followill, Jared Followill and Matthew Followill

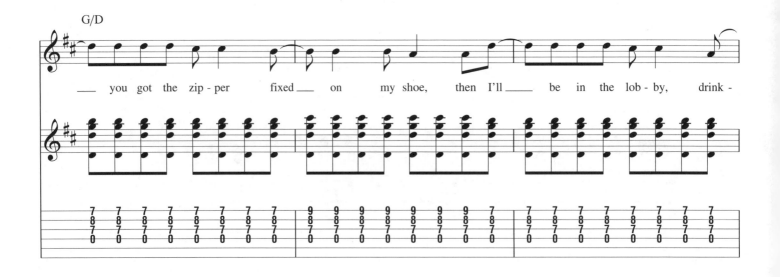

you got the zip-per fixed ___ on my shoe, then I'll ___ be in the lob-by, drink-

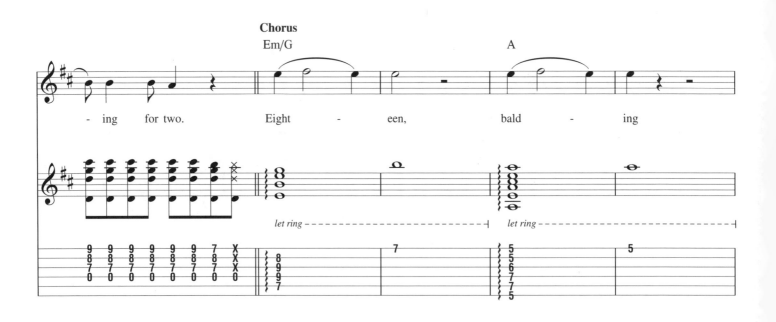

Chorus

-ing for two. Eight - een, bald - ing

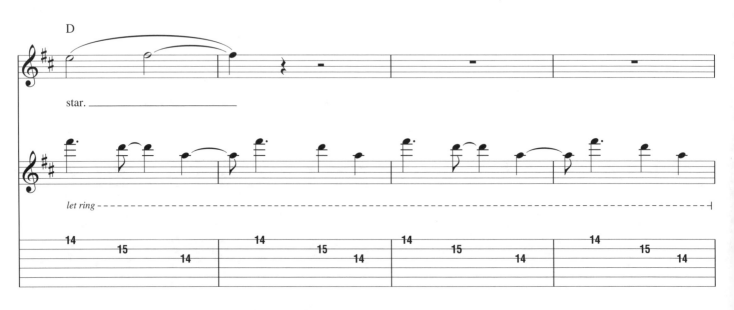

star. _____

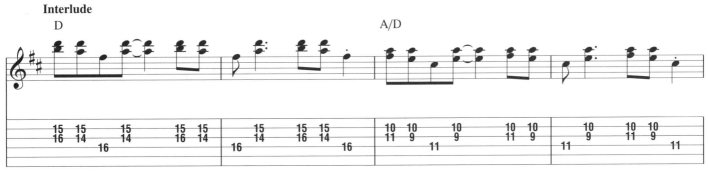

Additional Lyrics

2. Look at the shakies, what's with the blush?
   Fresh off the plane, in my fuzzy rush.
   Ev'ryone's gathered to idolize me,
   I hate the way you talk, your Japanese scream.
   It's been too long since I left the shed,
   You kick the bucket and I'll swing my legs.
   Always remember the pact that we made,
   Too young to die but old is the grave.

Pyro

Words and Music by Jared Followill, Matthew Followill, Nathan Followill and Caleb Followill

Intro
Moderately ♩ = 110

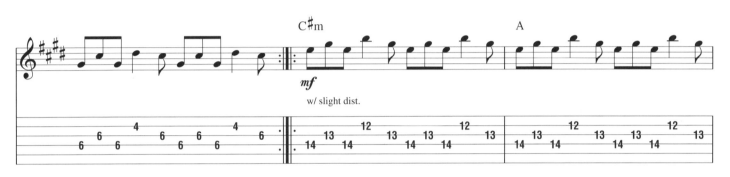

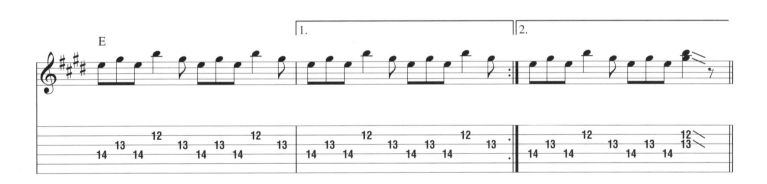

Verse

1. Sin - gle book ___ of match - es gon - na burn ___ what's stand - ing in ___ the way. ___
2. *See additional lyrics*

12

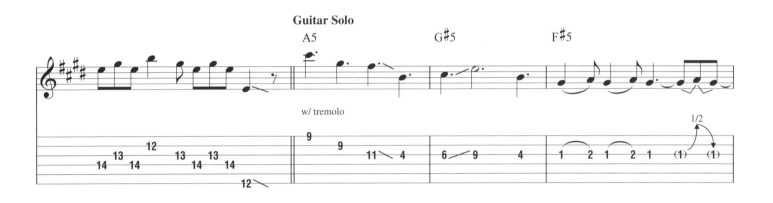

Guitar Solo

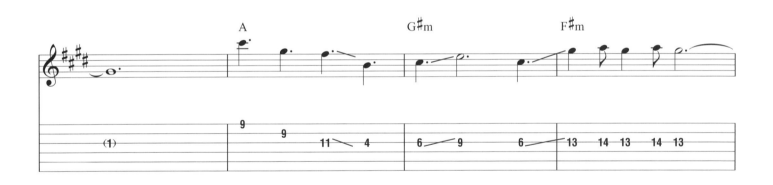

Bridge

Watch her roll. _____ Can you

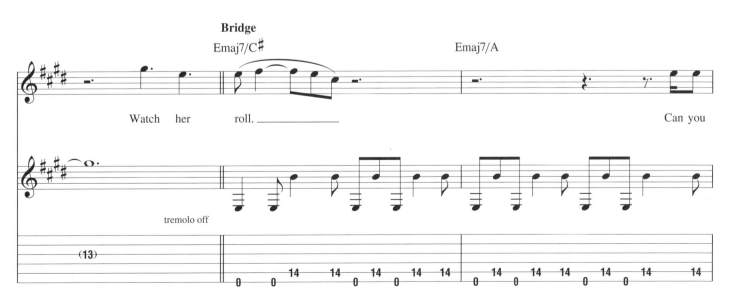

tremolo off

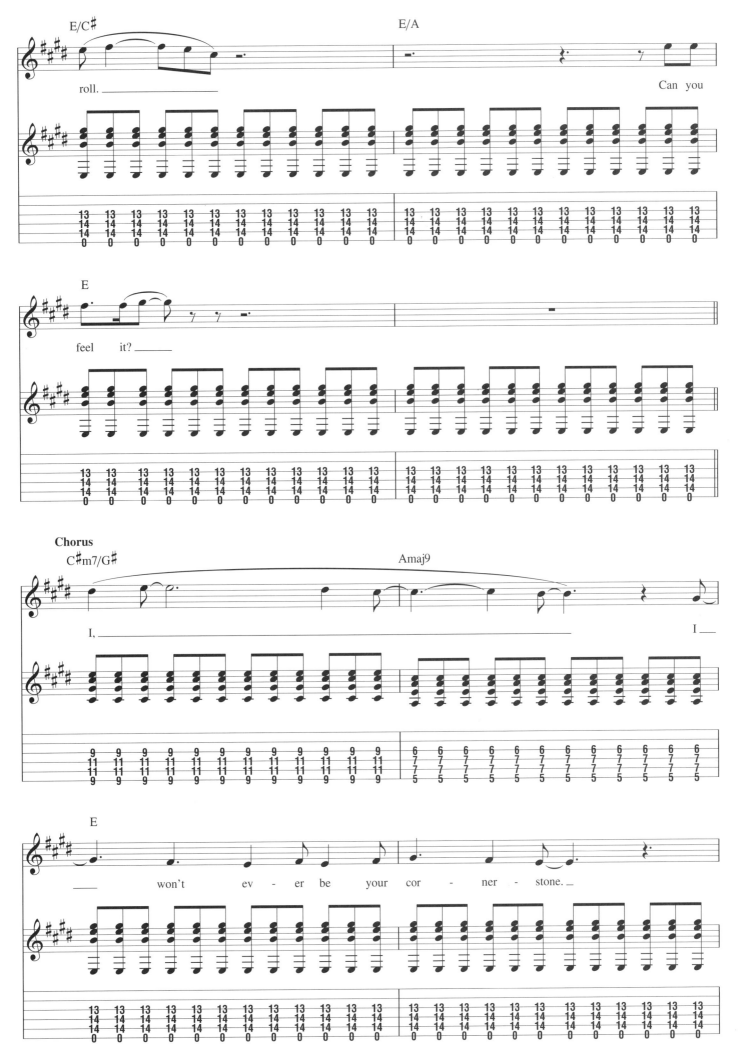

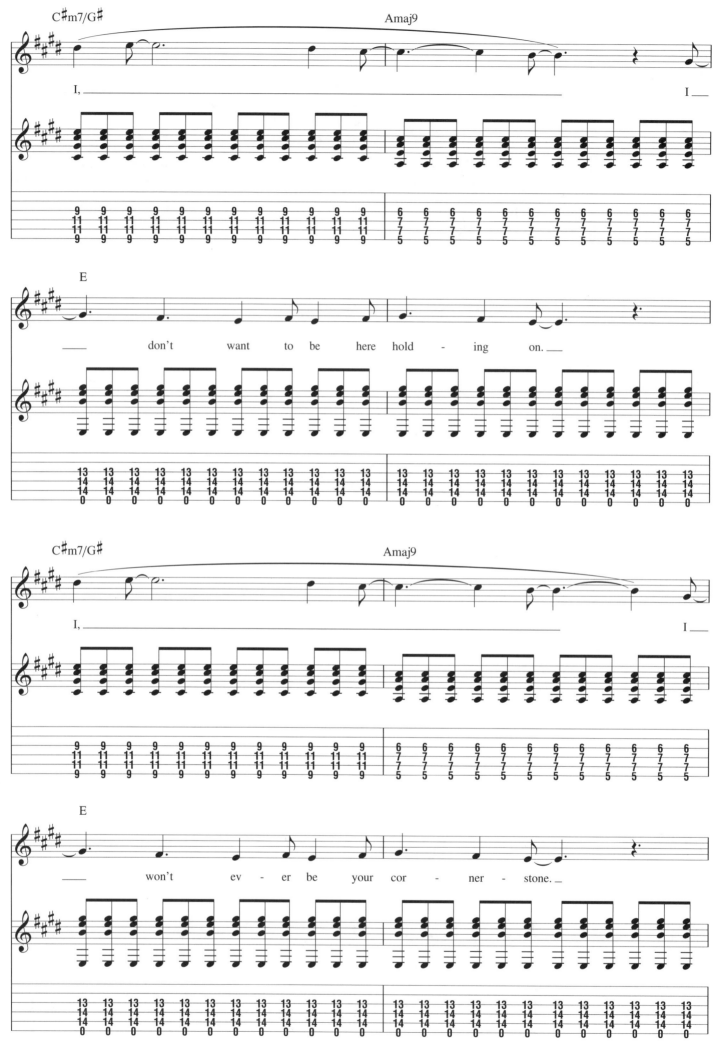

don't want to be here hold - ing on.

won't ev - er be your cor - ner - stone.

Additional Lyrics

2. All the black inside me is slowly seeping from the bone.
   Ev'rything I cherish is slowly dying or it's gone.
   Little shaken babies and drunkards seem to all agree.
   Once the show gets started it's bound to be a sight to see.

King of the Rodeo

Words and Music by Caleb Followill, Nathan Followill, Jared Followill and Matthew Followill

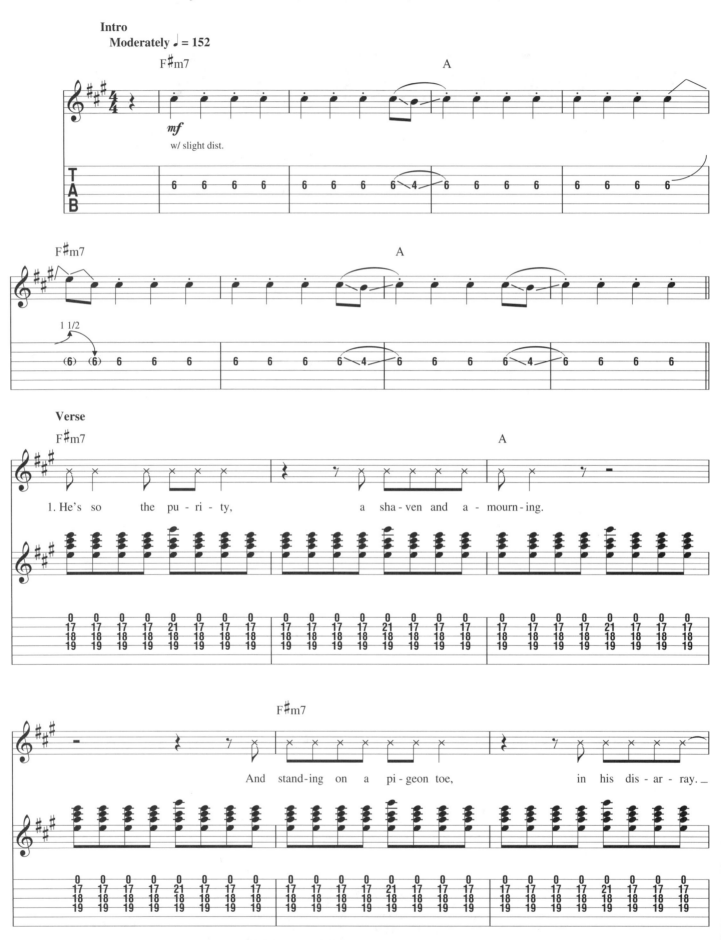

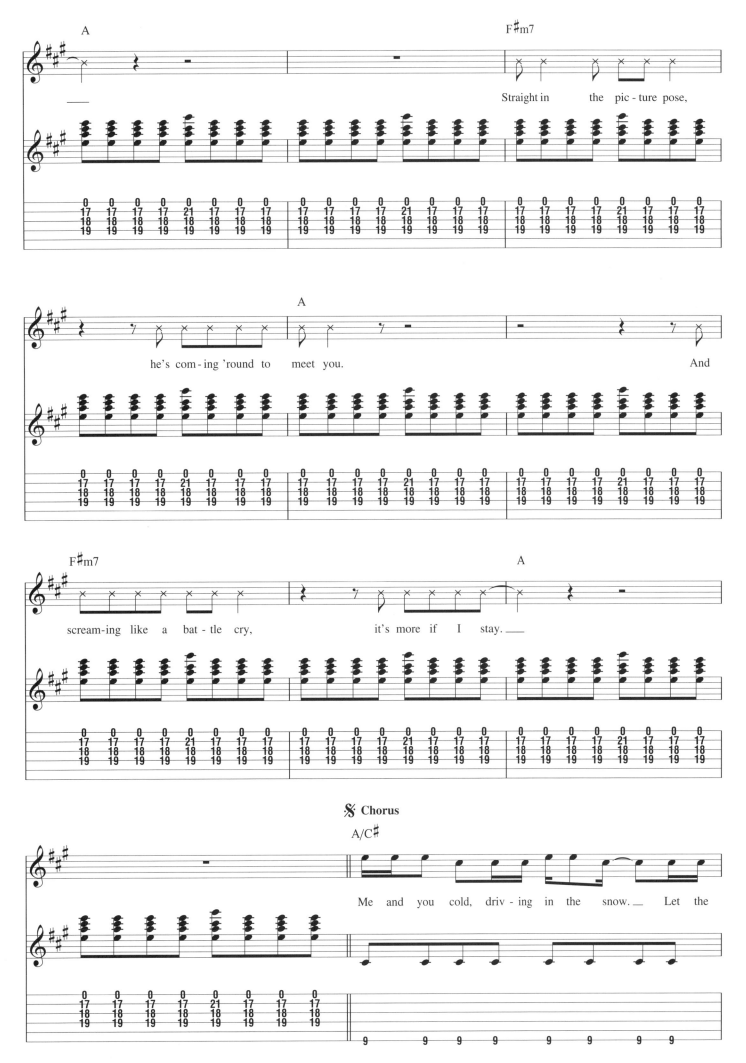

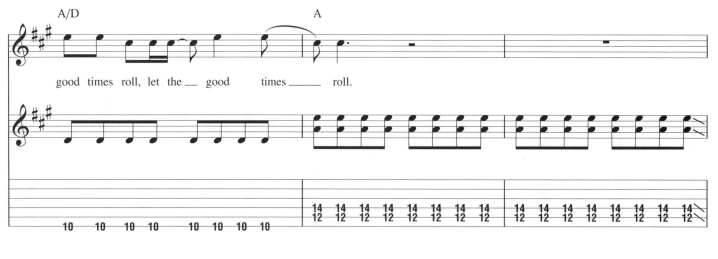

good times roll, let the __ good times __ roll.

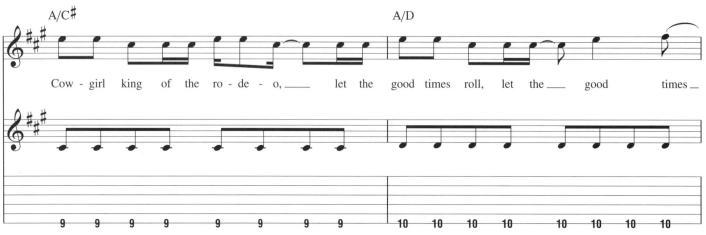

Cow - girl king of the ro - de - o, __ let the good times roll, let the __ good times __

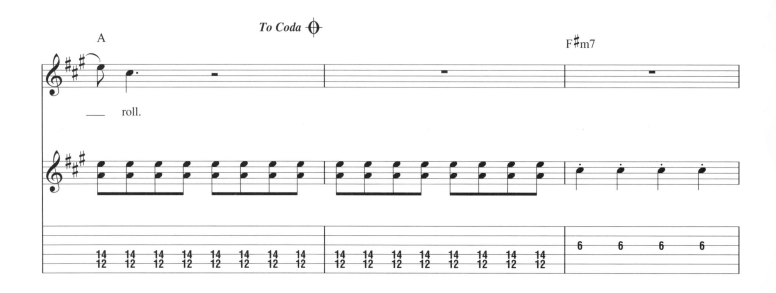

__ roll.

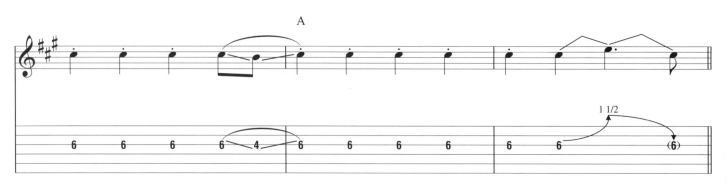

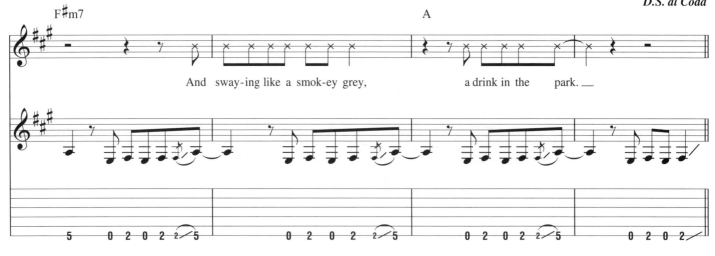

And sway-ing like a smok-ey grey, a drink in the park. __

Coda

Guitar Solo

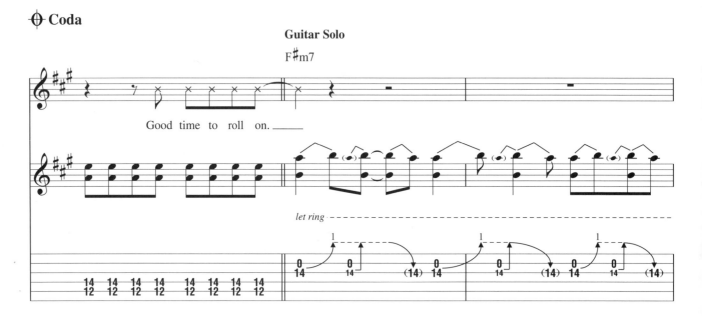

Good time to roll on. _____

let ring

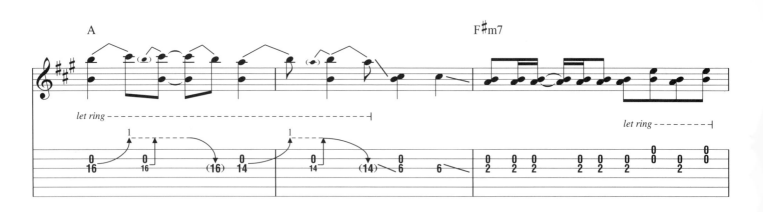

let ring

let ring

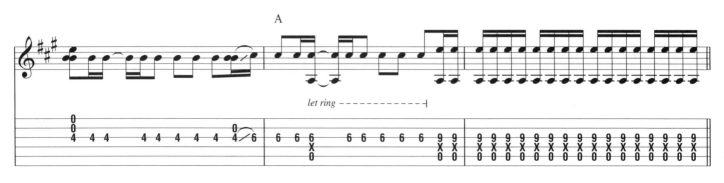

let ring

Outro

Good time to roll on. Good time to roll on. Good time to roll on.

Good time to roll on. Good time to roll on. Good time to roll on.

Good time to roll on. Good time to roll on. Good time to roll on.

On Call

Words and Music by Caleb Followill, Nathan Followill, Jared Followill and Matthew Followill

Intro
Moderately ♩ = 95

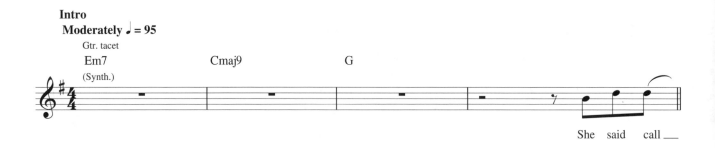

She said call ___

___ me now, ___ ba - by, I'd ___ come a run - ning.

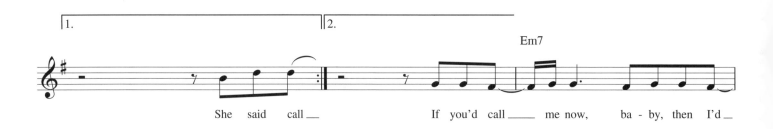

She said call ___   If you'd call ___ me now, ba - by, then I'd ___

Interlude
N.C.
(Bass)

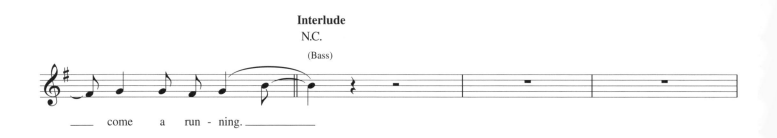

___ come a run - ning. ___

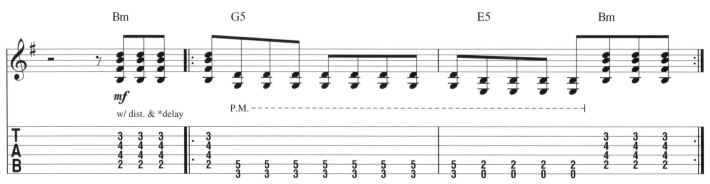

* Set for loud 16th note regeneration w/ 1 repeat.

Verse

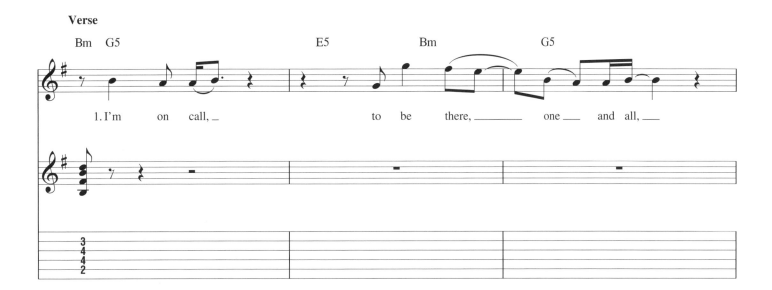

1.I'm on call, ___ to be there, ___ one ___ and all, ___

to be there, ___ when I fall ___ to piec - es, ___

Chorus

___ Lord, ___ you know, ___ I'll be there wait - ing.

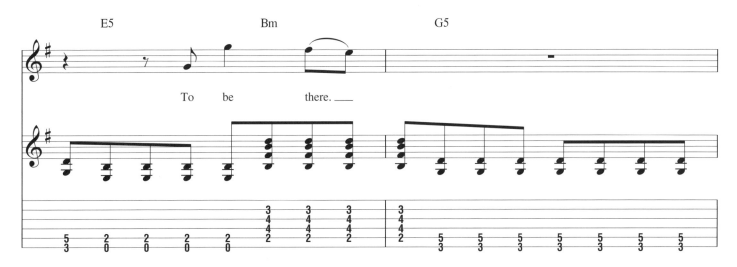

To be there. ___

Verse

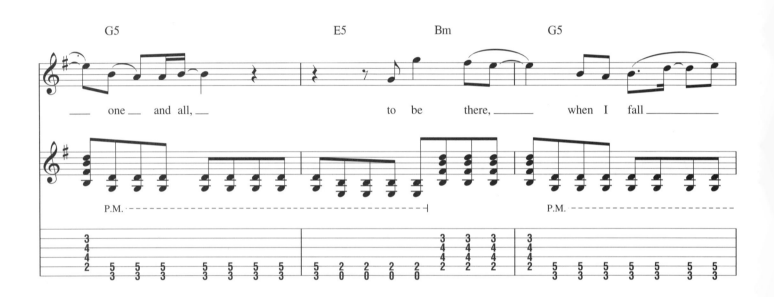

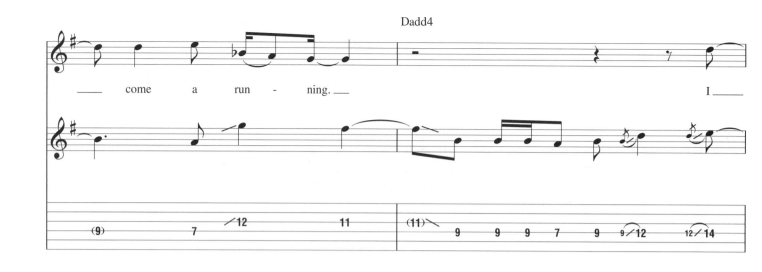

come a run - ning.

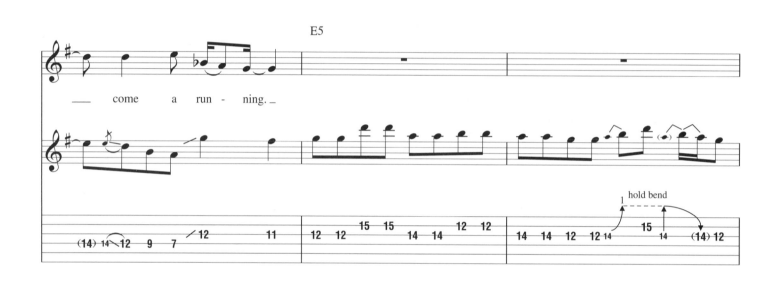

come a run - ning.

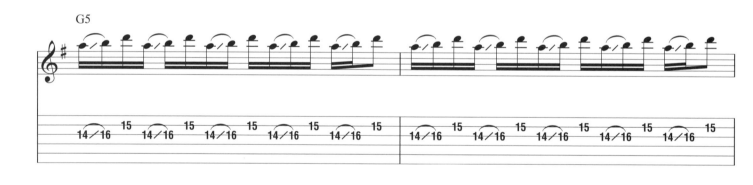

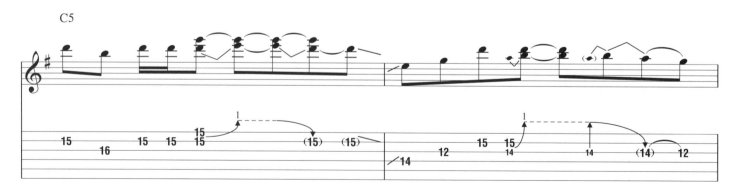

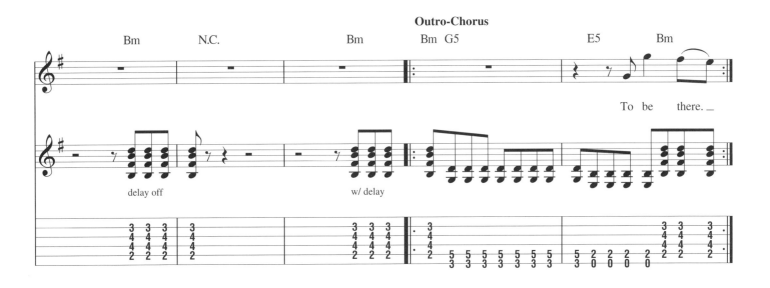

Red Morning Light

Words and Music by Caleb Followill, Nathan Followill and Angelo Petraglia

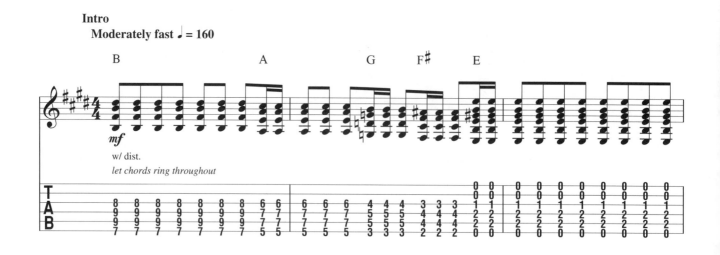

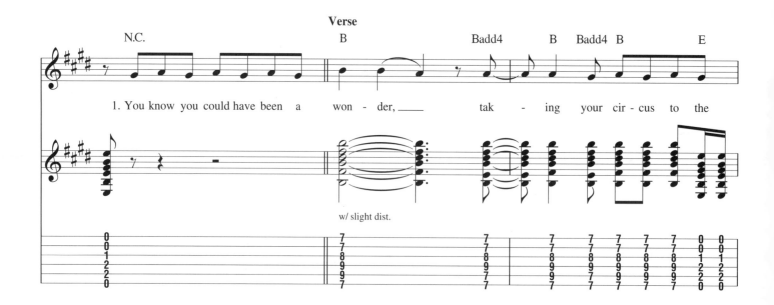

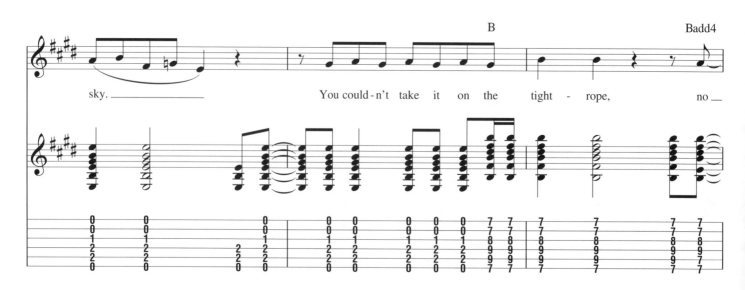

To Coda ⊕

32

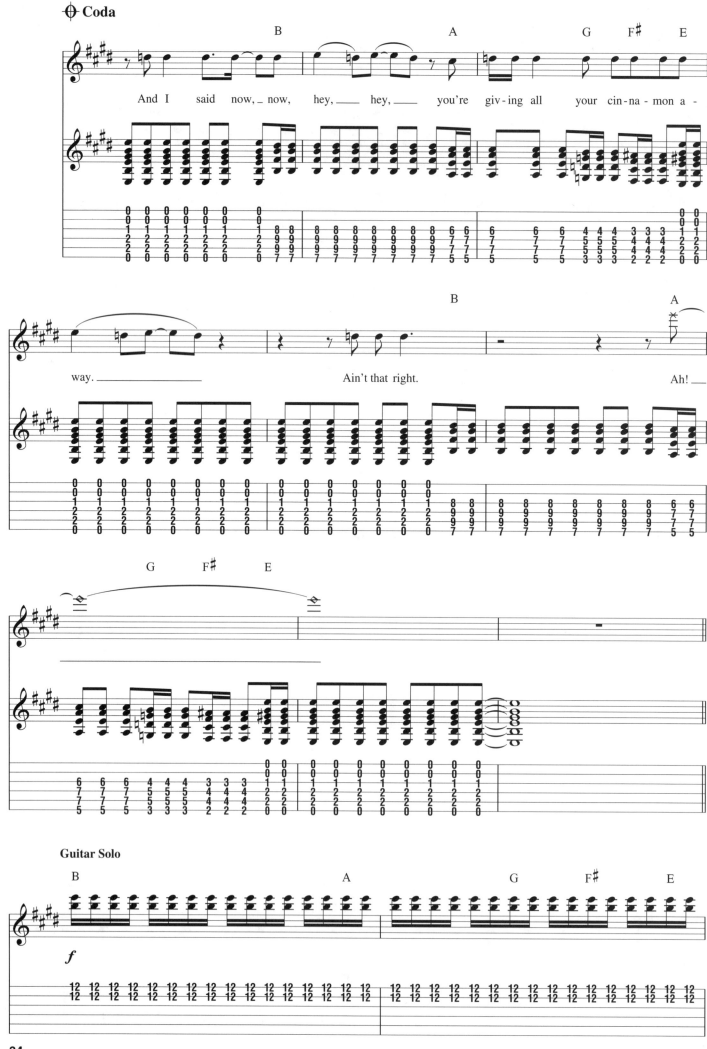

B

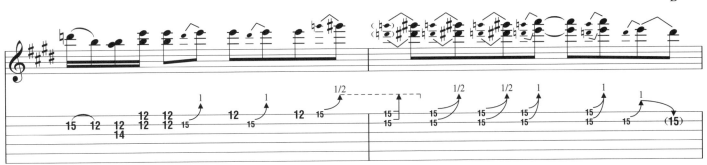

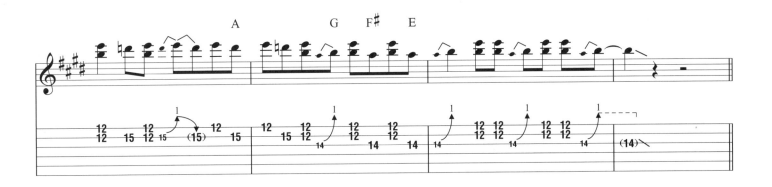

Interlude

Gtr. tacet
N.C.

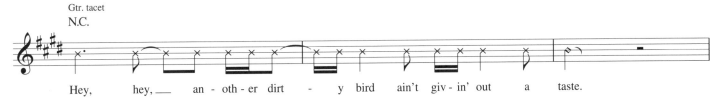

Hey, hey, __ an - oth - er dirt - y bird ain't giv - in' out a taste.

Oh, hey, keep on giv - ing a - way __ and giv - ing it a - way,

giv - ing it a - way. Well hey, hey, __ you're giv -

ing all your cin - na - mon a - way.   A

hey, hey, __ you're giv - ing all __ your cin - na - mon a - way.

35

way. _____ That's not right. Ow! _____

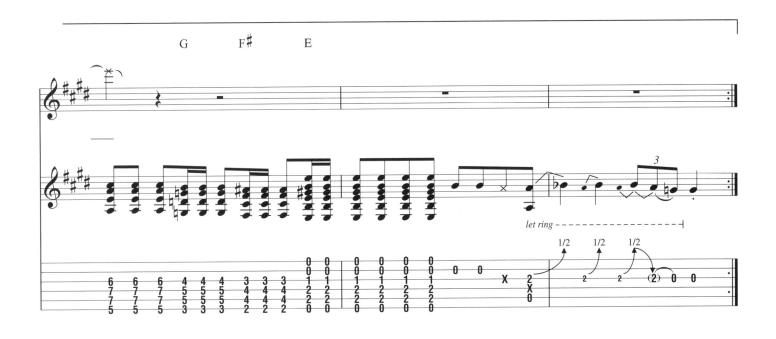

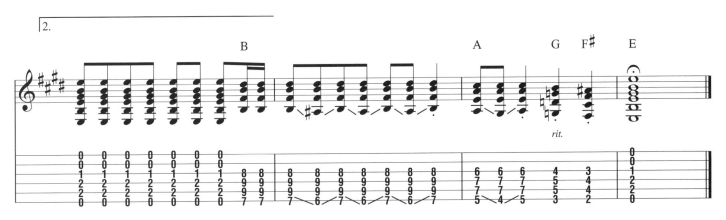

Sex on Fire

Words and Music by Caleb Followill, Nathan Followill, Jared Followill and Matthew Followill

your sex is on fire. _____

Con - sumed _____

with   what's   to   tran - spire. _____

3. Hot   as   a   fe-

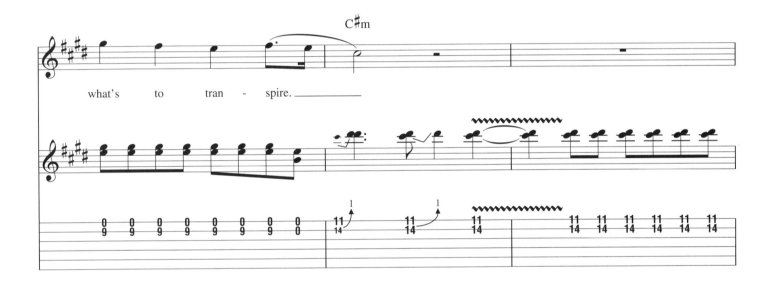

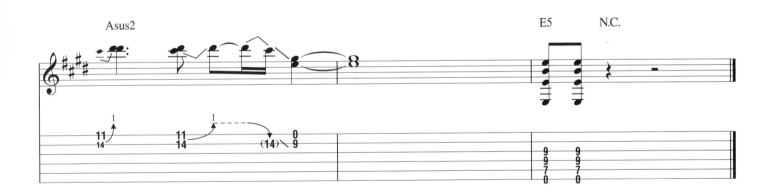

Additional Lyrics

3. Hot as a fever. Rattling bones.
   I could just taste it, taste it.
   If it's not forever, if it's just tonight,
   Oh, it's still the greatest, the greatest, the greatest.

Use Somebody

Words and Music by Caleb Followill, Nathan Followill, Jared Followill and Matthew Followill

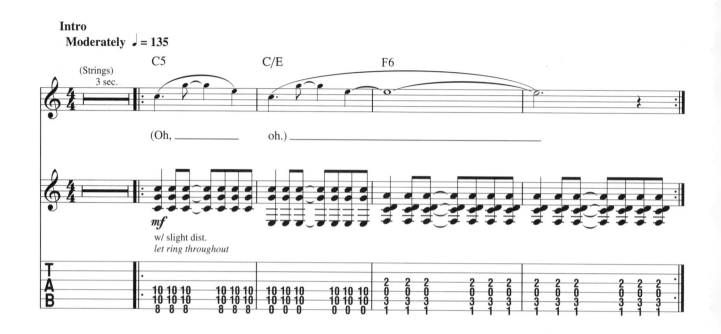

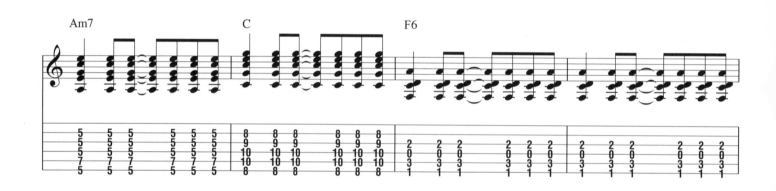

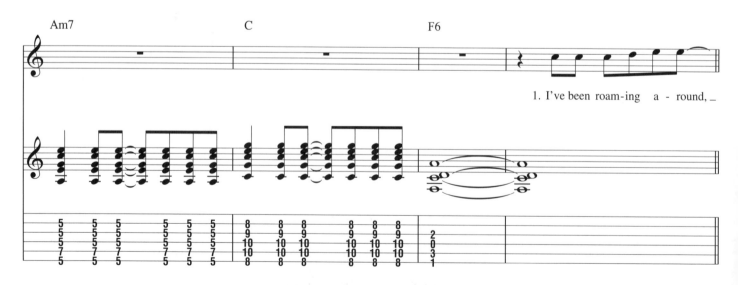

Verse
Gtr. tacet

while you live it up ____ I'm off ____ to sleep ____

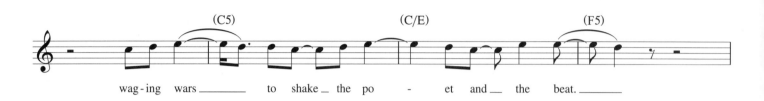

wag-ing wars ____ to shake __ the po - et and __ the beat. ____

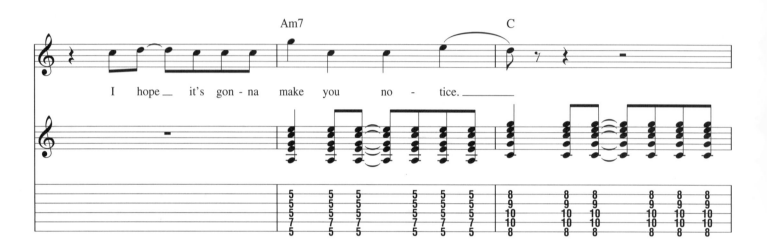

I hope __ it's gon-na make you no - tice. ____

I hope __ it's gon-na make you no - tice ____

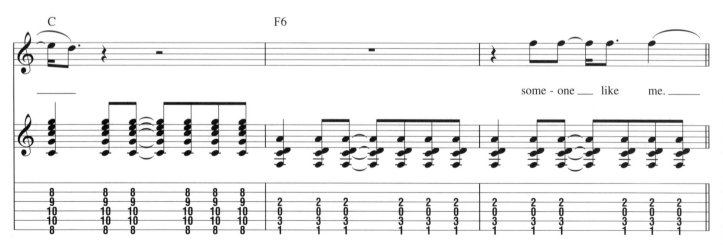

some - one __ like me. ____

Chorus

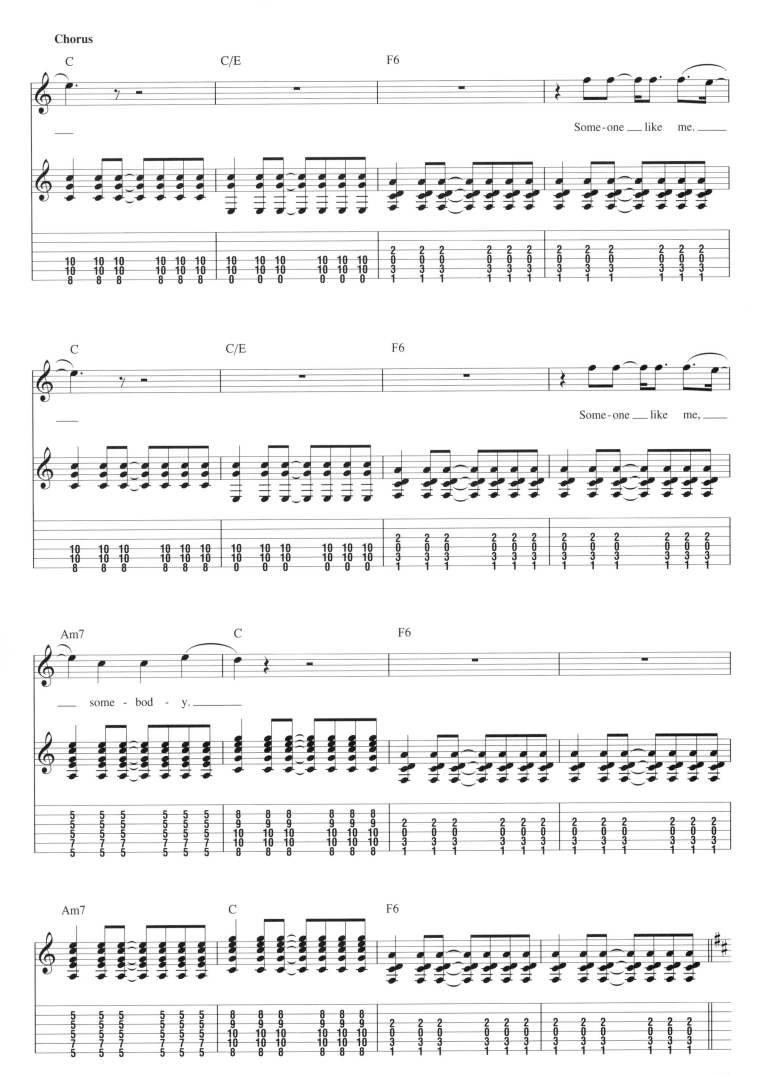

Bridge

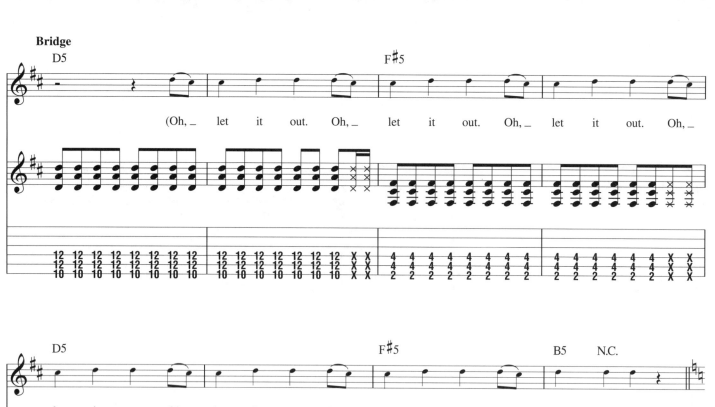

(Oh, _ let it out. Oh, _ let it out. Oh, _ let it out. Oh, _

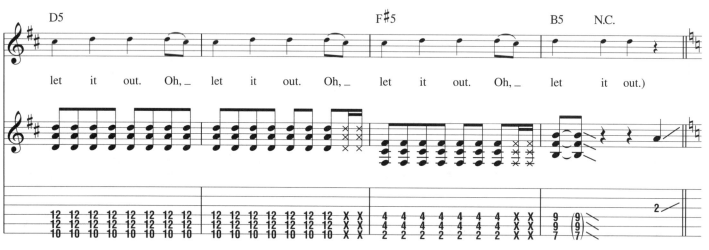

let it out. Oh, _ let it out. Oh, _ let it out. Oh, _ let it out.)

Interlude

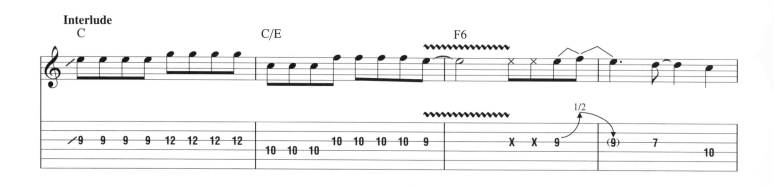

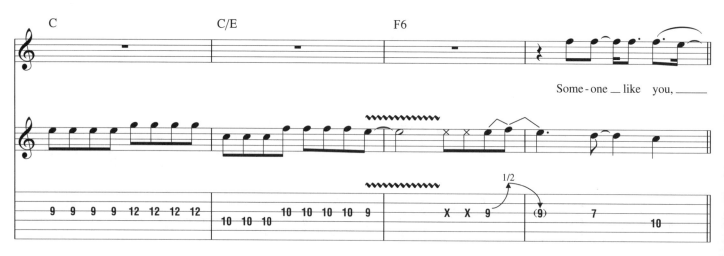

Some-one _ like you, _____

Radioactive

Words and Music by Jared Followill, Matthew Followill, Nathan Followill and Caleb Followill

Intro
Moderately ♩ = 128

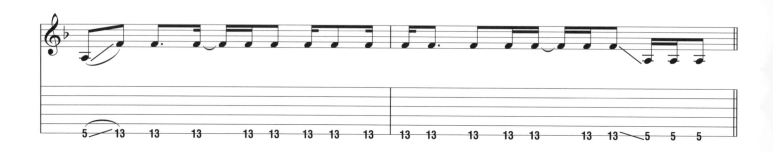

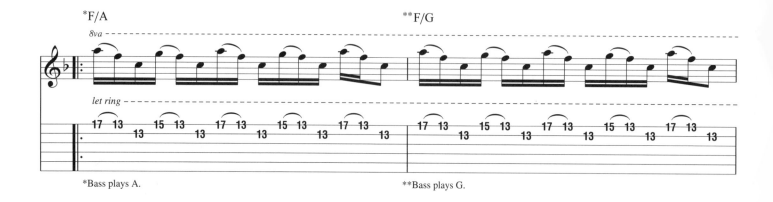

*Bass plays A.

**Bass plays G.

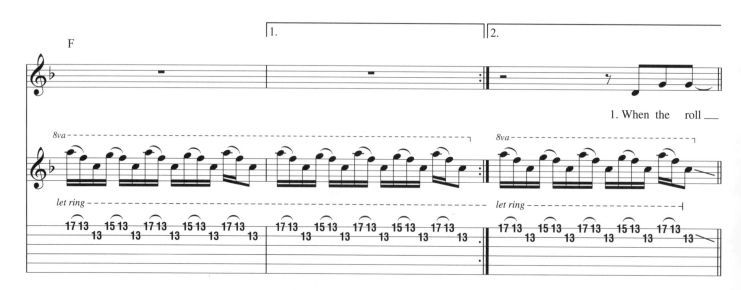

Chorus

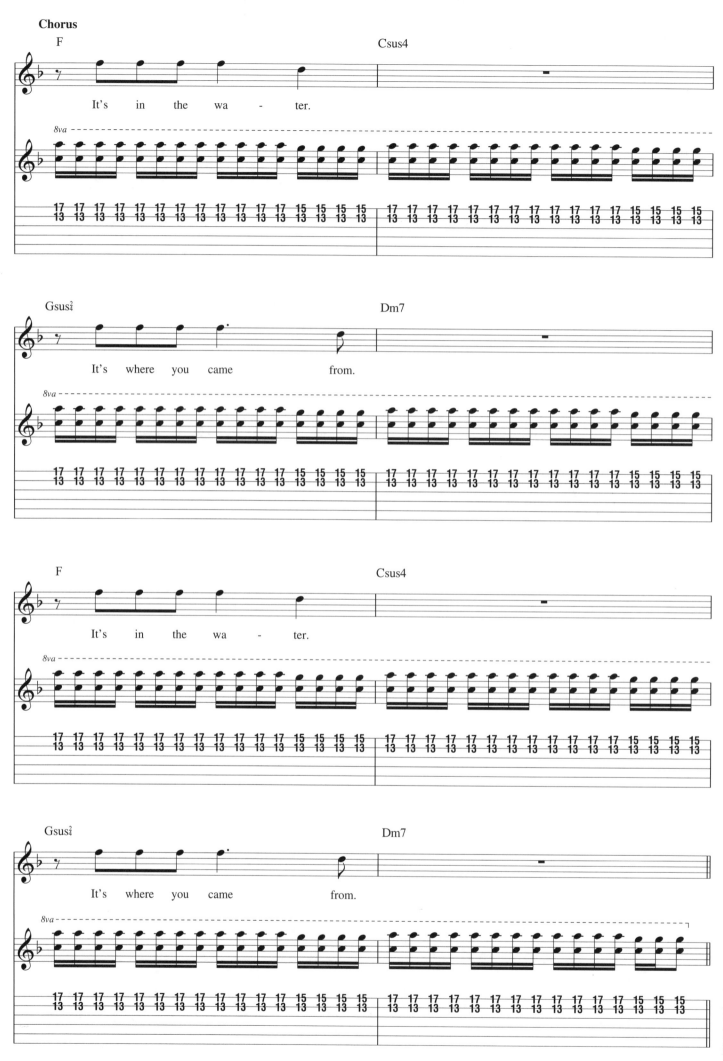

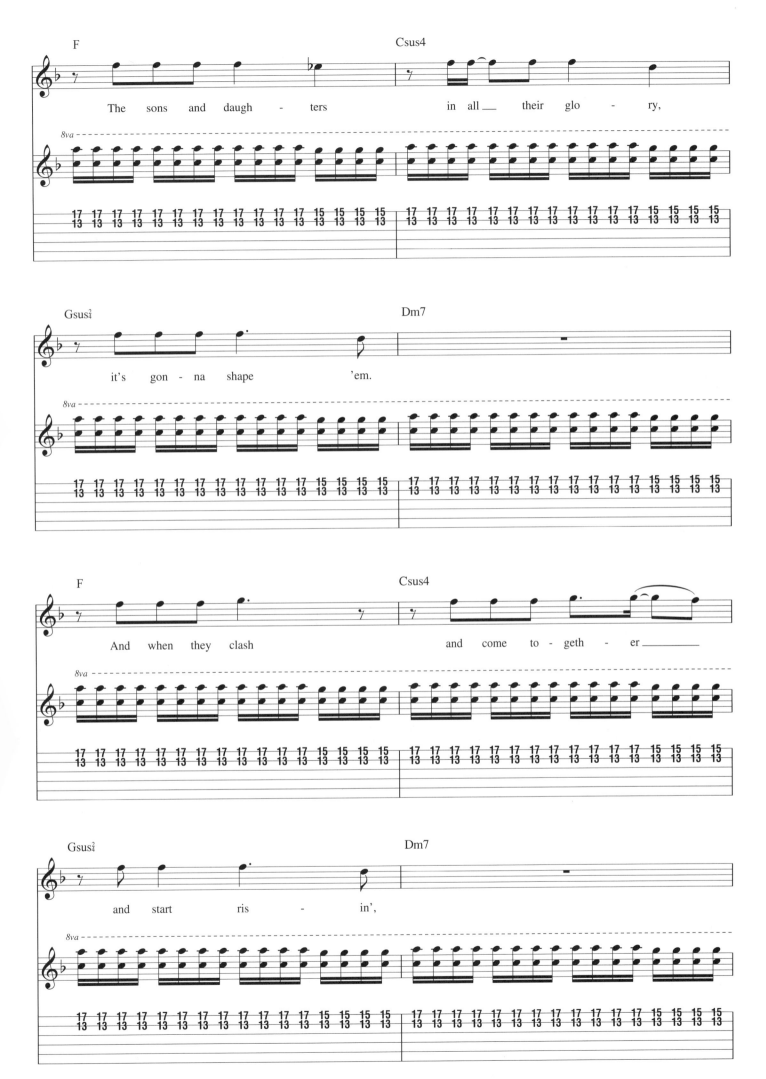

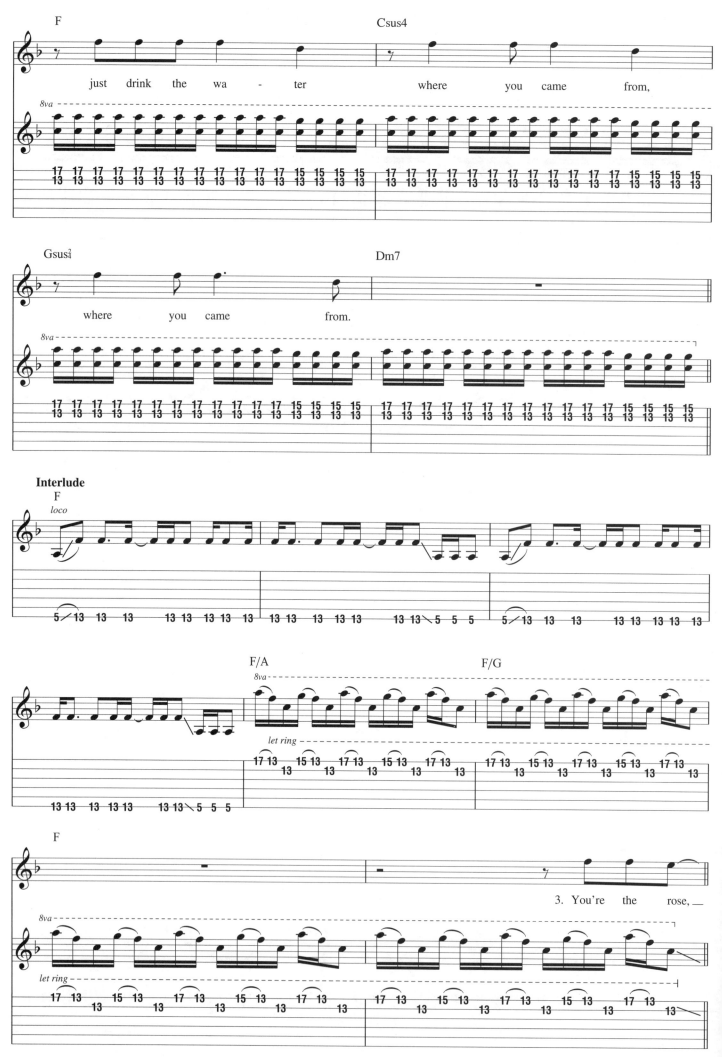

Chorus

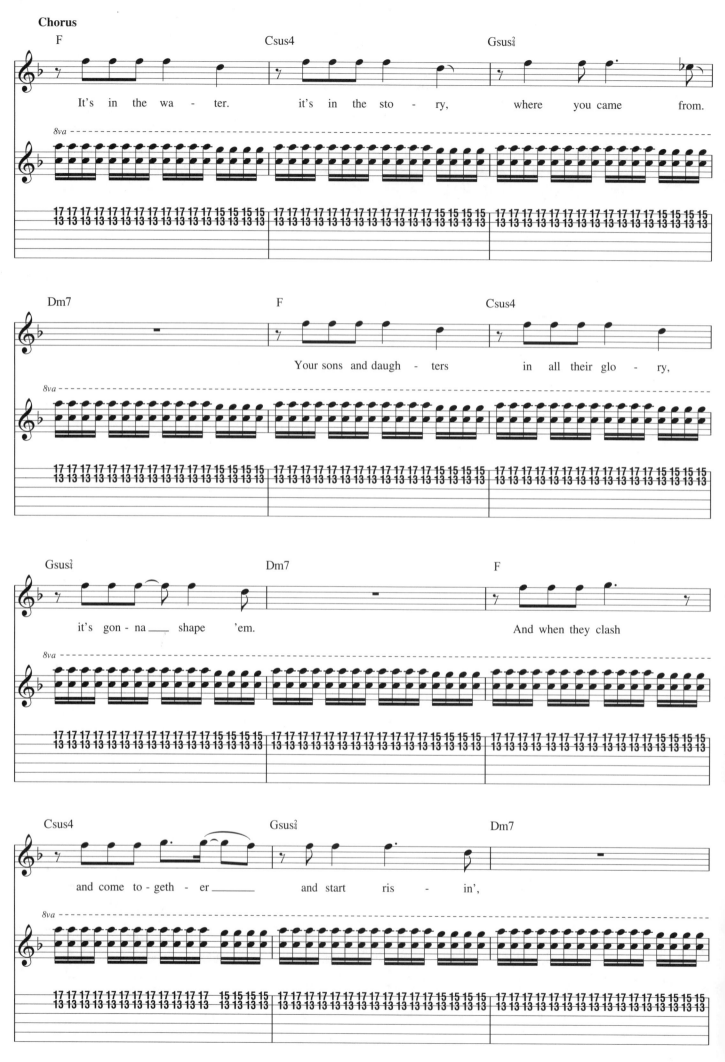

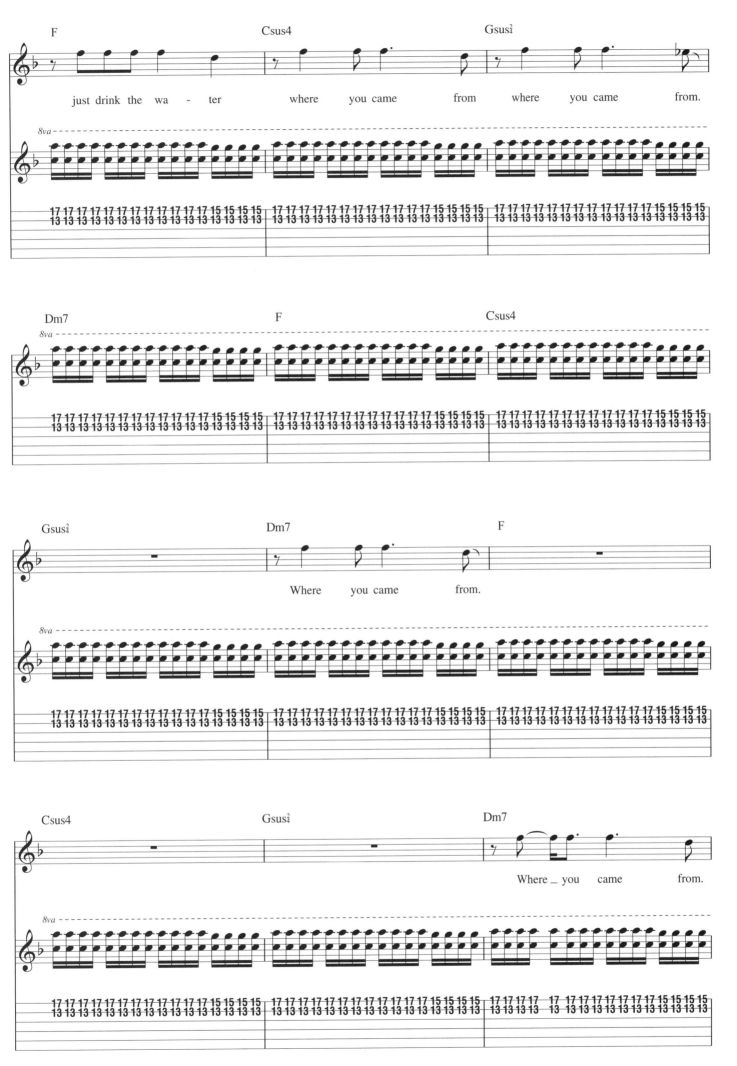